RETIREMENT BEYOND THE 401(k)

A Comprehensive Planning Guide
for GenXers Who Did It Their Way

Introduction: Rewriting the Retirement Script

Let's be honest. The word 'retirement' was invented by corporations and governments to describe what happens when you stop being useful to the economy. It assumes a lifetime of steady employment, decades of contributions to a 401(k), and a tidy pension waiting at the end. For a lot of us GenXers - the latchkey kids, the grunge survivors, the generation sandwiched between Boomers who got the gold and Millennials who got the attention - that script never quite fit.

Many of us made deliberate choices to reject the corporate grind. We freelanced, we hustled, we raised kids, we cared for parents, we made art, we built communities. We traded financial security for freedom, autonomy, and meaning. And now we're staring down the back half of our lives wondering: what does retirement even look like for us?

This guide isn't going to tell you to max out your Roth IRA (though if you can, great). It's going to ask bigger questions and help you answer them for your own life.

A Different Kind of Wealth

This guide operates on the premise that a good life in your later years depends on far more than money: community, purpose, food security, health, shelter, creativity, and joy. These are things you can build, tend, and grow at any income level.

Work through this guide section by section. Write in it. Share it with a partner, a friend, or your community. Use it as a map for the conversations you need to have with yourself and the people you love.

DISCLAIMER: I am not a financial advisor nor an expert on retirement. I'm just a GenXer trying to figure this all out and trying to help anyone feel better about their situation so they can make the most of their life circumstances. Please do your own due diligence with any information in this book. Websites may no longer exist and information can change.

Section 1 – Community: Your Most Valuable Retirement Asset

Across nearly every study of longevity and life satisfaction, one factor consistently outperforms wealth: the quality of your relationships. The Japanese concept of 'ikigai' (your reason for getting up in the morning) is almost always rooted in connection. Community isn't a luxury in retirement. It's infrastructure.

The bad news: many of us have let community erode. We moved for work, we scattered our social circles, we outsourced connection to social media. But also, we believed capitalists who convinced us to be "rugged individuals." The good news: community can be rebuilt, intentionally and beautifully.

Building Intentional Community

MUTUAL AID NETWORKS

Mutual aid is the original safety net: neighbors helping neighbors, no means-testing required. Many communities have formal mutual aid groups; if yours doesn't, you can start one. These networks provide practical support (food, childcare, transportation, home repair) while building the deep social bonds that make life rich.

- Find existing mutual aid groups in your area via Facebook, Nextdoor, or local nonprofits
- Offer a skill you have: cooking, driving, tech help, emotional support
- Host a neighborhood resource swap or skill share
- Create a shared resource list for your street or apartment building

CO-HOUSING AND INTENTIONAL LIVING

Co-housing communities are resident-designed neighborhoods where private homes cluster around shared spaces: kitchens, gardens, workshops, childcare. They dramatically reduce the cost of living while increasing social connection. Interest in co-housing among older adults has grown significantly, and GenX is well-positioned to pioneer new models.

- Research existing co-housing communities near you (cohousing.org is a good starting point)

- Consider forming a housing cooperative with trusted friends or community members

- Explore 'golden girls' style house-sharing arrangements

- Look into accessory dwelling units (ADUs) for multigenerational living

NEIGHBORHOOD AND LOCAL TIES

Knowing your neighbors isn't quaint; it's practical. Neighbors are who you call in an emergency. They watch your house, share their harvest, lend a hand when you're sick.

- Host a block party, potluck, or community dinner

- Join or start a neighborhood association or community garden

- Frequent local businesses and introduce yourself

- Volunteer with a local organization that matters to you

Reflect & Write

- Who are the five people you want to be closest to in the next chapter of your life?

- What community do you wish existed? Is there a way you could help create it?

- Where do you feel most a sense of belonging right now? How could you deepen that?

Section 2 – Housing: Where You'll Actually Live

Housing is the biggest variable in most people's financial lives and also an area where creativity and community can open doors that conventional thinking closes. The goal isn't necessarily to own a home free and clear (though that's wonderful if it's accessible to you). The goal is stability, comfort, and a place that serves your life.

Reimagining Where and How You Live

REDUCING HOUSING COSTS

- House hacking: rent out a room, basement, or ADU to offset your mortgage or rent
- Downsize intentionally. Less space often means more freedom and more money for experiences
- Relocate to a lower cost-of-living area, including rural communities, small cities, or abroad
- Explore rent-stabilized housing, housing cooperatives, or community land trusts
- Look into HUD programs, Section 8, and senior housing options if you qualify

NON-TRADITIONAL HOUSING OPTIONS

- Tiny homes: lower purchase price, lower utilities, smaller footprint
- Manufactured housing: often significantly cheaper than site-built homes
- RV or van dwelling: radical mobility and dramatically reduced overhead
- Land co-ops: shared land ownership with individual or small dwellings
- Cooperative apartments: you own a share in the corporation, not the unit itself
- Monasteries and intentional religious communities: some offer housing for lay residents

HOME MAINTENANCE AS COMMUNITY

If you own a home, deferred maintenance is a financial time bomb. Building relationships with neighbors who have complementary skills, and offering your own, can dramatically reduce costs and build the reciprocal community you'll want to rely on later.

- Create or join a neighborhood tool-lending library

- Organize work parties for big projects (painting, gardening, repairs)

- Learn basic home repair skills. YouTube is genuinely an excellent teacher

- Barter skills with local tradespeople

RENT VS. OWN: A MORE HONEST CONVERSATION

Homeownership has been sold as the cornerstone of the American Dream, but for many GenXers in high cost-of-living areas, renting may actually provide more financial flexibility. The key is stability: long-term leases, strong tenant protections, or low-rent areas where you can put down roots without a mortgage.

Reflect & Write

• Does your current housing serve the life you want in the next 10-20 years?

• What would your ideal living situation look like, not necessarily what you think is possible?

• Who would you want to live near, or with, in later life?

Section 3 – Food: Growing, Sharing, and Eating Well

Food security is one of the most fundamental aspects of a stable life and one of the most powerful places to opt out of systems that don't serve you. Growing even a small portion of your own food, participating in food-sharing networks, and building skills around cooking and preservation can dramatically reduce your cost of living while connecting you to land, seasons, and community.

Growing Your Own Food

STARTING A GARDEN

You don't need a lot of space or money to grow food. Container gardens on balconies, raised beds in small backyards, and community garden plots can all produce meaningful amounts of vegetables, herbs, and fruit.

- Start with what you eat most and what's easiest to grow in your climate
- Herbs (basil, mint, rosemary, thyme) are easy, productive, and save money immediately
- Tomatoes, zucchini, beans, and greens are productive for beginners
- Perennials like asparagus, rhubarb, and berry bushes reward patience with years of harvest
- Connect with local gardeners and cooperative extension services for region-specific advice

Did you know that SNAP benefits (as of the writing of this book) can be used to buy seeds and plants that product food? Eligible items include:

- Vegetable seeds and plants (e.g., tomatoes, peppers, lettuce)
- Fruit trees and berry bushes
- Edible roots, bulbs, and plants (e.g., asparagus crowns, onion bulbs)
- Herb plants and seeds used for cooking (e.g., basil, cilantro, mint)

COMMUNITY GARDENS AND FOOD FORESTS

Community gardens provide growing space to people without land, while food forests, multi-layered edible landscapes, offer produce to entire neighborhoods. Many cities have both, and many communities need people to help build and steward them.

- Search for community gardens in your area through your city's parks and recreation department
- Look for or help start a food forest with your local permaculture group
- Volunteer with urban farming organizations for skills and free produce

PRESERVING AND FERMENTING

Preserving food through canning, fermenting, drying, and freezing extends the harvest season and reduces waste. These skills, largely lost in recent generations, are deeply satisfying and highly practical.

- Start with simple ferments: sauerkraut, kimchi, yogurt, kombucha
- Learn water bath canning for high-acid foods (jams, tomatoes, pickles)
- Dehydrate fruits, vegetables, and herbs for shelf-stable snacks
- Freeze summer surpluses for winter meals

Food Sharing and Community

FOOD SWAPS AND GLEANING

- Organize neighborhood food swaps: your extra zucchini for their extra eggs
- Join gleaning organizations that harvest surplus from farms and orchards
- Participate in or start a neighborhood free pantry (Little Free Pantry model)
- Connect with Olio, Too Good To Go, and other food-sharing apps

COMMUNITY MEALS

Shared meals are one of humanity's oldest rituals of connection. Community suppers, potlucks, and neighborhood dinners build relationships while reducing the cost and effort of cooking every meal alone.

- Host a monthly potluck or community supper

- Cook in bulk and share with neighbors, especially elderly or isolated community members

- Look into community fridges, which offer free food in public spaces

- Volunteer at, or help organize, community meals through local faith communities or nonprofits

FORAGING

Wild food is free, nutritious, and connects you to the land in a profound way. Many common 'weeds' are edible: dandelion, purslane, wood sorrel, lamb's quarters. Fruit trees and berry bushes grow in public spaces in most cities.

- Take a local foraging walk with an experienced guide before eating anything wild

- Learn to identify 5-10 common edible plants in your region

- Use apps like iNaturalist and Falling Fruit to identify plants and find public harvests

Reflect & Write

- What's one food skill you'd like to develop or deepen in the next year?

- How could you make food a way of building community in your life?

- What does 'food security' feel like to you, and how close are you to it?

Section 4 – Health & Body: Caring for the Machine You Live In

Healthcare is one of the most anxiety-inducing aspects of retirement planning for GenXers, especially those who've spent years without employer-sponsored insurance. Many were thankfully able to take advantage of the ACA. But physical and mental health are also deeply shaped by things money can't buy: movement, sleep, connection, purpose, time in nature, and freedom from chronic stress.

Preventive Health and Lifestyle

MOVEMENT AS MEDICINE

Exercise is probably the single most powerful tool available for aging well, and it's largely free. Walking, cycling, swimming, dancing, yoga, gardening, and strength training all support longevity, mental health, and independence.

- Walk at least 30 minutes a day, ideally outdoors and with company
- Find movement you genuinely enjoy: dance, hiking, martial arts, pickleball, swimming
- Strength training twice a week reduces falls and loss of function with age
- Yoga and stretching support flexibility, balance, and stress reduction
- Community sports, group fitness classes, and walking clubs combine movement with connection

SLEEP

Chronic sleep deprivation accelerates aging, impairs memory, and significantly increases the risk of cardiovascular disease, diabetes, and depression. Sleep is essential maintenance.

- Prioritize 7-9 hours of sleep consistently
- Reduce alcohol, which disrupts sleep architecture
- Magnesium and castor oil (taken orally or topically) can improve sleep quality
- Create a wind-down routine: dim lights, screens off an hour before bed
- Address sleep apnea if you snore or wake feeling unrefreshed

MENTAL HEALTH AND EMOTIONAL WELLBEING

GenX was largely raised to be self-sufficient to a fault. Many of us learned to suppress emotional needs and push through pain. In later life, this catches up with us. Investing in emotional health now - through therapy, community, creativity, and reflection - is investing in your quality of life.

- Seek therapy or counseling if you're carrying unresolved grief, trauma, or anxiety
- Community mental health centers often offer sliding-scale fees
- Peer support groups offer connection and shared experience at no cost
- Mindfulness and meditation practices can reduce anxiety and depression
- Open Path Collective and other directories connect people with affordable therapists

Navigating Healthcare Without a Net

UNDERSTANDING YOUR OPTIONS

- If you're under 65: explore ACA marketplace plans, especially if your income is low enough for subsidies
- Medicaid covers low-income adults in states that expanded coverage
- Community health centers offer sliding-scale care regardless of insurance status
- Dental schools provide reduced-cost dental care
- GoodRx, Mark Cuban's Cost Plus Drugs, and similar services dramatically reduce prescription costs
- Telehealth services have expanded access for routine and mental health care
- LGBTQ+ elders face specific discrimination risks in healthcare and elder care settings — SAGE (sageusa.org) provides advocacy, resources, and a national helpline specifically for LGBTQ+ older adults

WHEN YOU TURN 65

Medicare becomes available at 65 regardless of work history. Understanding your Medicare options before you need them is genuinely important, and Medicare rights organizations offer free counseling.

- Research Medicare Parts A, B, C (Medicare Advantage), and D well before 65

- State Health Insurance Assistance Programs (SHIP) offer free, unbiased Medicare counseling

ALTERNATIVE AND COMPLEMENTARY CARE

Acupuncture, herbal medicine, chiropractic, and other modalities are increasingly accessible and sometimes covered by insurance. Community acupuncture clinics offer sliding-scale treatments in group settings.

MEDICAL TOURISM

Medical tourism (traveling to another country for healthcare) has moved well beyond the fringes. Millions of Americans seek care abroad every year, driven almost entirely by cost. For people without adequate insurance coverage, or facing procedures with five-figure price tags in the US, it deserves serious consideration rather than dismissal.

The savings can be staggering. Dental work, elective surgery, orthopedic procedures, eye surgery, and even cancer treatment can cost 50 to 80 percent less in countries like Mexico, Costa Rica, Thailand, Portugal, and Colombia, often at internationally accredited hospitals with English-speaking staff trained at Western medical schools. The quality gap that Americans assume exists frequently does not.

What people commonly seek abroad:

- Dental care: implants, crowns, full-mouth restorations — dental tourism alone saves Americans an estimated $3,000 to $15,000 per visit compared to US prices

- Vision care: LASIK and cataract surgery at a fraction of US cost

- Orthopedic surgery: hip and knee replacements, rotator cuff repair

- Cardiovascular procedures, cancer treatment, and fertility treatments

- Prescription medications: many drugs are available over the counter or at dramatically lower prices in Mexico and other countries

Popular destinations and what they're known for:

- Mexico (especially Los Algodones, Tijuana, and Monterrey): dental, vision, medications, orthopedics — extremely popular due to proximity and low cost

- Costa Rica: dental and cosmetic surgery, with strong reputation for quality and easy travel from the US

- Thailand: world-class hospitals in Bangkok with internationally accredited facilities and full-spectrum care

How to do it safely:

- Research accreditation: look for hospitals and clinics accredited by Joint Commission International (JCI), the international equivalent of US hospital accreditation

- Get referrals and read reviews from other patients, not just provider websites — expat forums and medical tourism communities are invaluable

- Plan for recovery time abroad: many procedures require you to stay in-country for follow-up care before flying home

- Get all records and documentation translated and in hand before returning home

- Identify a US-based doctor willing to handle follow-up care before you go, not after

- Consider travel insurance that covers medical complications abroad

Reflect & Write

• What's one health habit you know you should build? What's stopped you?

• How is your emotional and mental health right now, honestly?

• What healthcare gaps keep you up at night? What's one step toward addressing them?

Section 5 – Money & Resources: Making the Most of What You Have

Let's talk about money - without shame, without judgment, and without the assumption that you should have done things differently. You made the choices that made sense at the time. Now let's look at what you have, what you need, and what you can do. And if you're reading this in a moment of genuine crisis rather than planning, the 211 helpline and the BenefitsCheckUp tool in the resources section are good places to start.

This section is not financial advice. It's an invitation to get clear on your actual financial picture and start making intentional choices.

Getting Clear on Your Numbers

INCOME STREAMS

Retirement income doesn't have to come from a single source. Map out every possible stream:

- Social Security (find out where you're at by visiting ssa.gov)
- Full time, part-time or flexible work you actually enjoy
- Rental income from a room, ADU, or property
- Creative work: writing, art, music, crafts
- Freelance consulting in your field
- Teaching skills you have that you can use to teach online courses, community workshops, and/or tutoring
- Pension, IRA, or 401(k) distributions if you have them
- Dividend income from investments if applicable

REDUCING EXPENSES

The most powerful retirement lever you have may not be income; it may be expenses. The gap between what comes in and what goes out determines your freedom.

- Audit your recurring expenses: subscriptions, insurance, utilities, food, transportation

- Reduce or eliminate car ownership if public transit, cycling, or walking is viable (As a bonus, if this is feasible, it also keeps you healthy.)
- Move to a lower cost-of-living area if your current location is straining your budget
- Embrace the sharing economy: libraries, tool libraries, clothing swaps
- Develop skills that replace paid services: cooking from scratch, basic repairs, sewing

BENEFITS YOU MAY NOT KNOW ABOUT

- SNAP (food stamps): eligibility thresholds may be higher than you think
- LIHEAP: federal assistance with heating and cooling costs
- Property tax exemptions for seniors and low-income homeowners
- Lifeline: reduced-cost phone and internet for qualifying low-income households
- Medicare Extra Help: reduces prescription costs for low-income Medicare beneficiaries
- Veterans benefits: if you served in the military, the VA offers healthcare, disability compensation, pension programs, and other benefits that are significantly underused — visit va.gov or call 1-800-698-2411 to find out what you qualify for
- 211: if you or someone you know is in crisis, 211 is the national helpline connecting people to local food, housing, healthcare, and emergency assistance — available by phone and at 211.org
- BenefitsCheckUp.org: comprehensive screening tool for programs you may qualify for

Alternative Economic Models

THE GIFT ECONOMY AND TIME BANKING

Time banking replaces dollars with hours: your hour of tutoring is worth the same as an hour of plumbing. Time banking networks exist in many cities and offer a way to exchange services without money. The gift economy, giving freely and trusting in reciprocity, goes even further.

- Search hOurworld.org or TimeBanks USA for networks in your area
- Look into local Buy Nothing groups, which operate on radical gift exchange

Worker cooperatives, consumer cooperatives, and credit unions prioritize members over shareholders. Choosing cooperative institutions, especially credit unions over banks, keeps more money in your community.

- Move your banking to a local credit union

- Shop at food co-ops when possible

- Explore worker co-ops if you're still working or considering new work

Reflect & Write

• What does your actual financial picture look like right now: income, expenses, debts, assets?

• What benefits or programs might you be leaving on the table?

• What's one expense you could reduce or eliminate without meaningfully impacting your quality of life?

Section 6 – Purpose & Meaningful Work: What Gets You Out of Bed?

One of the least-discussed crises of conventional retirement is the loss of purpose. For people whose identity was bound up in their career, retirement can feel like falling off a cliff. But for those of us who never fully subscribed to the work-is-identity model, there's an opportunity here: to get intentional about what gives our lives meaning.

Ikigai: Your Reason for Being

Ikigai is a Japanese concept that roughly translates to 'reason for being' or 'reason to get up in the morning.' It sits at the intersection of four things: what you love, what you're good at, what the world needs, and what you can be compensated for. The compensation doesn't have to be money. It can be reciprocity, recognition, or the simple satisfaction of contribution.

- What could you do for hours without noticing time passing?
- What do people consistently come to you for help with?
- What problems in your community feel urgent and solvable?
- What work, paid or not, feels most alive to you?

Volunteering and Service

Volunteering in later life has been consistently linked with better physical and mental health, longer life, and greater life satisfaction. It's also one of the most powerful ways to build community and find purpose.

- Choose causes that genuinely matter to you, don't just fill a schedule
- Look for leadership opportunities in volunteer roles, not just task-filling
- AmeriCorps Seniors programs offer small stipends for older adults doing community service; at the current time (2026), this program has been defunded but may return
- Mentor younger people in your field, craft, or community

Creative Work and Making

Making things - whether it's bread, music, furniture, quilts, stories, or code - is one of humanity's most sustaining activities. Many GenXers suppressed their creative lives during the work-and-raise-kids years. This is your time to reclaim them.

- Return to a creative practice you set aside
- Join a maker space, writing group, choir, band, or community theater
- Explore whether your creative work could generate modest income: Etsy, local markets, commissions
- Teach your craft through workshops, YouTube, or community centers
- Create for the joy of it, without attaching the value to whether it sells

Continued Learning

Many community colleges and universities offer free or deeply reduced tuition to older adults. Learning new skills, exploring new subjects, and engaging your curiosity are all powerful antidotes to the cognitive decline associated with isolation and passivity.

- Research senior audit programs at local colleges and universities
- Explore free online learning: Coursera, edX, Khan Academy, MIT OpenCourseWare
- Take up a skill that requires learning in community: language, instrument, chess
- Join or start a book club, discussion group, or lecture series

Reflect & Write

- What would you do with your days if money were no object and you had no obligations?

- What's something you've always wanted to learn or create but haven't made time for?

- Where do you feel most useful or most needed in your community?

Section 7 – Environment & Place: Where You Belong in the World

Where you live shapes almost everything: your cost of living, your access to community, your health, your sense of belonging, and the natural world you inhabit. Choosing your place intentionally - or getting clear on why you're staying where you are - is one of the most important retirement decisions you can make.

Evaluating Where You Live

WALKABILITY AND TRANSPORTATION

As we age, car dependence becomes increasingly precarious - financially, physically, and socially. A walkable neighborhood with good public transit is genuinely a quality-of-life asset worth a great deal.

- Use Walk Score (walkscore.com) to evaluate your current neighborhood's walkability
- Consider proximity to grocery stores, healthcare, and community spaces
- Evaluate public transit options: bus, train, bike share
- Consider a bicycle, which dramatically extends the range of car-free living

CLIMATE AND ENVIRONMENTAL FACTORS

Climate change is rapidly reshaping which places are livable long-term. Extreme heat, wildfire risk, flooding, and water scarcity are all legitimate factors in long-term location decisions.

- Research climate vulnerability for your current and potential future locations
- Consider the long-term implications of water availability, especially in Western U.S.
- Evaluate wildfire and flood risk carefully before buying or renting property
- Urban heat islands disproportionately harm older adults without air conditioning

Rural areas often offer dramatically lower costs of living, space for gardening and animals, and communities with strong mutual aid traditions. They also come with trade-offs: less access to healthcare, fewer cultural amenities, and sometimes social isolation.

- Small cities and college towns often combine affordability with urban amenities

- Some areas actively recruit remote workers and retirees with incentive programs

- Research broadband availability, which is increasingly essential for remote work, maintaining social connections, and telehealth

Nature and the Outdoors

Access to green space, water, and natural landscapes has significant positive effects on mental and physical health. Time in nature reduces cortisol, improves mood, boosts immune function, and fosters a sense of connection that goes beyond human community.

- Prioritize daily time outdoors, even in urban areas

- Learn the plants, birds, and ecosystems of where you live

- Volunteer with trail maintenance, conservation organizations, or parks

- Consider proximity to parks, trails, water, and green space in housing decisions

Reflect & Write

- Does where you live serve your values and your vision for the next chapter?

- What is your relationship with the natural world and what would you like it to be?

- If you could live anywhere, where would it be, and what's actually stopping you?

Section 8 – Relationships: The Heart of Everything

We've already talked about community in the broad sense. This section is about the intimate relationships that form the emotional core of a good life: partnerships, friendships, family, and your relationship with yourself.

Partnership and Intimate Relationships

If you're in a partnership, retirement - or the approach of it - is a stress test. Financial pressure, changing roles, health challenges, and shifting identities can strain even solid relationships. It's worth investing in intentional conversations long before crisis hits.

- Have honest conversations about money, expectations, and vision for the future
- Discuss how much time you want to spend together vs. separately
- Address health decisions and end-of-life wishes explicitly (see Section 10)
- Consider couples counseling as a tune-up, not a last resort
- If you're single, be honest about what you want: partnership, community, or both

Friendship: The Underrated Essential

Friendship is one of the biggest casualties of busy adulthood. Maintaining and building friendships in later life requires intentionality, but the payoff is enormous. Close friendships are among the strongest predictors of happiness and longevity.

- Invest in existing friendships: regular calls, visits, letters, shared experiences
- Make new friends through shared interests, volunteer work, and community involvement
- Be the person who initiates: call, invite, show up
- Friendship takes vulnerability; risk being honest about what you need

Family of Choice

Not everyone has warm biological family relationships. For many GenXers, especially LGBTQ+ members, estranged family members, or those who simply built their closest bonds outside blood ties, chosen family is the real family. These relationships deserve the same intentionality and investment as any other.

- Be explicit with your chosen family about what you mean to each other

- Build rituals and traditions that honor those relationships

- Consider legal protections: healthcare proxies, wills, and beneficiary designations should reflect your actual family

Your Relationship with Yourself

Perhaps the most important work of the second half of life is the ongoing project of knowing yourself: what you actually want (not what you were told to want), what gives you joy, what causes you suffering, and what you're willing to change.

- Journaling, therapy, and contemplative practices all support self-knowledge

- Learn to distinguish between 'I can't' and 'I've decided not to'

- Practice gratitude not as toxic positivity, but as honest attention to what is good

- Make peace with the past - not by minimizing it, but by integrating it

Reflect & Write

- Who are the most important relationships in your life? Are you investing in them?

- What do you wish people knew about what you need in relationships?

- What's your relationship with yourself like? What would you want to change?

Section 9 – Spiritual & Inner Life: What Sustains You?

Spirituality doesn't require religion, though for many people, religious community is a profound source of connection and meaning. At its core, spiritual life is about your relationship with what's larger than yourself: nature, time, mystery, love, beauty, mortality. The second half of life often calls us into deeper engagement with these questions, whether we're ready or not.

Meaning and Mortality

Death is the great taboo of modern secular culture and the thing we most need to make peace with. People who have honestly grappled with their mortality consistently report greater appreciation for life, clearer priorities, and less anxiety. Contemplating the end is how we figure out how to live.

- Read "Being Mortal: Medicine and What Matters in the End" by Atul Gawande, "Die Wise: A Manifesto for Sanity and Soul by Stephen Jenkinson," or similar works
- Attend a Death Café: free community conversations about death and dying
- Complete your advance directive and share it with the people who need it
- Write an ethical will: the values and wisdom you want to leave behind

Contemplative Practice

Meditation, prayer, time in nature, ritual, and contemplative reading are all ways of cultivating inner quiet and resilience. These practices have deep roots in nearly every human culture and have strong evidence behind them for reducing stress and improving wellbeing.

- Start a simple meditation practice: even 10 minutes daily makes a difference
- Apps like Insight Timer offer free guided meditations from many traditions
- Explore the traditions that resonate with you: Buddhist, Indigenous, Hindu
- Create personal rituals: morning pages, evening walks, seasonal celebrations

Connection to Something Larger

Whether through religious community, environmental activism, artistic expression, or service to others, the experience of being part of something larger than yourself is deeply sustaining. Finding it, or deepening your existing connection, is worth significant effort.

- Explore or deepen a spiritual or religious community if that calls to you

- Environmental work can provide a powerful sense of contribution to future generations

- Ancestor work - exploring your family history and honoring those who came before - can be profoundly grounding

- Creative work, at its deepest, connects us to something beyond ourselves

Reflect & Write

- What sustains you when things are hard?

- How do you relate to your own mortality and is there work to do there?

- Where do you feel most connected to something larger than yourself?

Section 10 – Legal & Practical: The Boring Stuff That Actually Matters

Nobody loves this section. But skipping it can cause real harm to the people you love and real chaos in your life if something goes wrong. These aren't just documents; they're acts of care for your community and your chosen family.

Essential Documents

ADVANCE HEALTHCARE DIRECTIVE / LIVING WILL

This document specifies your wishes for medical care if you can't speak for yourself. It's also one of the most profound acts of love you can offer people who might otherwise face impossible decisions on your behalf.

- Designate as a healthcare proxy (medical power of attorney) someone who knows your values and will advocate for you
- Be specific about what interventions you do and don't want
- Share copies with your healthcare proxy, your doctor, and any close family members
- Free templates are available at CaringInfo.org

WILL AND ESTATE PLANNING

A will ensures your stuff goes where you want it to go. Without one, your state decides, and your state doesn't know about your chosen family, your values, or your wishes.

- Even a simple will is better than none
- Legal aid organizations provide free or low-cost wills to qualifying low-income adults
- Online services like FreeWill.com offer basic will creation at no cost
- Name beneficiaries on all financial accounts and insurance policies; these override your will

DURABLE POWER OF ATTORNEY

A durable power of attorney designates someone to handle financial and legal decisions if you're incapacitated. Choose someone you trust deeply as this is significant authority.

DIGITAL LIFE

What happens to your email, social media, and digital files when you die? This is a 21st-century question that most people haven't answered.

- Create a secure document listing your important accounts, passwords, and wishes

- Designate a legacy contact on Facebook and Google

- Include instructions for any digital assets: cryptocurrency, online accounts, intellectual property

Social Security Planning

The timing of when you claim Social Security significantly affects your lifetime benefit. If you can afford to wait, claiming later results in higher monthly payments. But there's no single right answer — it depends on your health, your other income, and your circumstances.

- Create an account at ssa.gov to see your earnings record and projected benefit

- Understand the trade-offs of claiming at 62 vs. full retirement age vs. 70

- If you're divorced and were married 10+ years, you may be entitled to a spousal benefit; visit the Social Security website (ssa.gov/family) for more info

- Consider consulting a Social Security claiming specialist

Reflect & Write

- Which of these documents do you have in place? Which are missing?

- Who would you want making decisions for you if you couldn't make them yourself?

- Have you had explicit conversations with the people in your life about your wishes?

____

____

____

____

____

____

____

Section 11 – Joy, Play & Rest: Because That's the Whole Point

Here's the thing about all those productivity gurus who talk about optimizing your retirement: they're missing it. The point of a good life isn't to be efficient. It's to be alive. Joy, play, rest, beauty, laughter, and delight are not rewards for getting everything else right. They are the thing itself.

What Do You Actually Enjoy?

Many of us have spent so long in survival mode working, parenting, caregiving, getting through that we've lost touch with what we actually enjoy. Reconnecting with joy is a practice, and it starts with paying attention.

- Keep a 'joy log' for a week: notice what moments light you up, even briefly
- Remember what you loved as a child; many of those loves are still there
- Say yes to things you'd normally decline, at least occasionally
- Make time for what you love before life makes it impossible

Play

Adults don't play enough. Play is not frivolous. It's how humans process stress, build connection, and access creativity. Games, sports, music, theater, improv, dancing, and building things are all forms of play that belong in a full adult life.

- Join a game night, trivia league, or book club
- Take up a sport you've always been curious about: pickleball, disc golf, kayaking, roller derby
- Play music, even badly
- Build something with your hands: woodworking, knitting, origami, Lego
- Improv comedy classes are genuinely excellent for developing presence and playfulness

Rest and Solitude

In a culture that equates busyness with virtue, rest is a radical act. Real rest, not just collapsing in front of the TV, but intentional restoration, is essential for health, creativity, and joy. Solitude, similarly, is not loneliness: it's the practice of being at home with yourself.

- Protect time in your week that has no agenda

- Practice napping without guilt

- Read for pleasure; not self-improvement, just pleasure

- Spend time in nature without your phone

- Sit with quiet long enough to hear your own thoughts

Travel and Adventure

Travel doesn't have to be expensive to be transformative. Exploring your own region, house-sitting abroad, Workaway and WWOOF programs, and traveling slowly rather than expensively all offer profound experiences without the price tag of conventional tourism.

- Explore your own region through day trips, camping, and local tourism

- Look into Workaway, HelpX, or WWOOF for accommodation-in-exchange-for-work travel opportunities

- Platforms like TrustedHousesitters.com offer free stays in exchange for pet care

- Senior travel programs and group trips can offer companionship and logistics support

Reflect & Write

- When did you last do something purely for the joy of it?

- What would you do more of if you had more time?

- What does rest genuinely feel like for you and are you getting enough of it?

Section 12 – Putting It All Together: Your Life Map

You've now thought about community, housing, food, health, money, purpose, place, relationships, spirituality, practicalities, and joy. That's your whole life. Now let's integrate it.

The Wheel of Life

Rate your current level of satisfaction in each of the following areas on a scale of 1-10. Then rate how important each area is to you. The areas where importance is high and satisfaction is low are your priority zones.

Life Area	Satisfaction (1-10)	Importance (1-10)	Priority?
Community & Belonging			
Housing & Shelter			
Food & Nourishment			
Health & Body			
Money & Resources			
Purpose & Work			
Environment & Place			
Relationships			
Spiritual & Inner Life			
Legal & Practical			
Joy, Play & Rest			
Learning & Growth			

Your Top Three Focus Areas

Based on your wheel of life, identify your top three priority areas. For each one, write one concrete action you will take in the next 30 days.

Reflect & Write

- Priority Area 1: ____

Action in next 30 days: ____

- Priority Area 2: ____

Action in next 30 days: ____

- Priority Area 3: ____

Action in next 30 days: ____

Your Vision Statement

In your own words: what does a good life look like for you in the next 10-20 years? Not the financial plan — the life plan. Who is there? Where are you? What are you doing? What matters?

Reflect & Write

- Write your vision freely — this is for you, not anyone else.

- What would have to be true for you to feel like you lived well?

- What's one thing you know you need to stop waiting for permission to do?

____

____

____

____

____

Section 13 – Your Circle: Building a Retirement Support Group

You've spent this entire guide doing some of the most honest thinking a person can do: what do I actually have, what do I actually need, and what kind of life do I actually want? Now consider doing it with other people.

The challenges in this guide are not yours alone. Your friends, siblings, former colleagues, and chosen family are almost certainly navigating versions of the same terrain: the same gaps between what was promised and what arrived, the same questions about housing and health and purpose and money. Most of them are doing it in isolation, the way GenX does everything: quietly, independently, and without asking for help.

A retirement support circle changes that. It's not a therapy group or a financial planning seminar. It's a small group of people who trust each other enough to be honest, committed enough to show up, and creative enough to start building real solutions together. The goal isn't commiseration. It's collective intelligence and mutual aid applied to the specific problem of figuring out the second phase of your life.

Who to Invite

Smaller is better to start. Four to eight people is an ideal range: big enough to bring diverse skills and perspectives, small enough that everyone can speak and be heard. Think about people who share your general values, your approximate life stage, and your willingness to be real. You don't need people who are all in the same financial situation. In fact, a mix of circumstances often produces the most creative solutions.

- Close friends who already know your real situation
- Siblings or other family members who are in a similar life stage and open to honest conversation
- Former colleagues or creative collaborators you've trusted over the years
- Neighbors or community members who share your values and your stage of life
- Members of your chosen family who you want in this chapter of your life regardless of biology

A note on who not to invite, at least to start: people who will perform positivity instead of being honest, people who will dominate rather than listen, and people whose primary relationship to difficulty is denial. This group only works if people are willing to show up as they actually are.

How to Start the Conversation

The hardest part is usually the first message. Many people feel embarrassed to admit they're thinking hard about retirement, or that they don't have it figured out. The invitation works best when it's honest and low-pressure: you're not asking people to confess their finances or commit to a co-housing commune. You're asking them to have a conversation.

A simple framing that works:

> *"I've been doing some real thinking about what the next chapter of my life looks like, and I realized I don't want to figure it out alone. I'd love to get a small group of people I trust together a few times a year to talk honestly about where we are and what we're building. No agenda, no pressure, just real conversation. Would you be in?"*

Share this guide with the people you invite. It gives everyone a common vocabulary and a shared framework before the first meeting, so you're not starting from scratch.

Running Your First Meeting

The first meeting has one job: establish trust and set the tone. Keep it simple. Feed people. Make it feel like the gathering of friends it is, not a committee meeting. Two to three hours is about right.

Suggested First Meeting Structure

- First, talk about and agree on confidentiality. What's said here stays here, unless someone explicitly says otherwise. People need to trust that their personal information will not be repeated.

- Then have a simple check-in: each person answers "Where am I right now, honestly?" in five minutes or less. No advice, no cross-talk. Just listening.

- Inventory the group's collective resources: what skills, knowledge, assets, connections, and capacities does this group have between them? Make a shared list. You'll be surprised.

- Identify the one or two areas where the group has the most shared concern: housing, healthcare, money, isolation, purpose. These become your first working topics.

- Set your basic agreements: how often you'll meet, where, etc.

- Close with one concrete thing each person will do before the next meeting, even if it's small: complete the Wheel of Life in this guide, research a co-housing option, look into a benefit they've been meaning to apply for.

What to Do in Ongoing Meetings

Meeting 2-4 times a year is enough to maintain meaningful momentum without it becoming another obligation. Each gathering can have a different focus, rotating through the topics that matter most to the group. Some ideas:

Skills and Resource Mapping

Go deeper on what the group collectively knows and has. One person is a nurse. Another owns a house with a large yard. Someone else has been budgeting creatively for twenty years and knows every assistance program in the county. Another person has a truck and mechanical skills. These assets, made visible and shared, are the beginning of a genuine mutual aid network. Make a living document the group can update.

Scenario Planning

Work through real scenarios together. What happens if one member of the group has a health crisis with no insurance? What if someone loses their housing? What if a member needs to move closer to family? Talking through these possibilities in advance, when there's no emergency, lets you build responses that are thoughtful rather than reactive. This is what mutual aid actually looks like in practice.

Dream Sessions

Not every meeting needs to be problem-solving. Sometimes the most valuable thing is giving each person space to say what they actually want without immediately running into the wall of what seems possible. Dreams, spoken aloud in front of people who care about you, have a way of becoming more real. And sometimes someone in the group knows exactly how to help make one happen.

Accountability Check-ins

Revisit the commitments from the previous meeting. Not to shame anyone who didn't follow through, but to troubleshoot: what got in the way, and can the group help remove that obstacle? Having witnesses to your intentions is a quietly powerful motivator.

Practical Things Your Circle Might Build Together

Over time, a circle of four to eight committed people can do things that none of them could do alone. The following are real possibilities, not fantasies, and all have been done by groups of ordinary people who decided to stop waiting for institutions to solve their problems.

- A shared tool library and repair co-op, so no one needs to own everything alone
- A shared garden plot or community growing space, reducing food costs and increasing connection
- A bulk buying cooperative for food, household supplies, or even healthcare costs
- A caregiving rotation for members who experience health crises, so no one faces illness alone or relies entirely on paid care
- A housing cluster: members who live near each other or intentionally relocate to the same neighborhood or co-housing community
- A shared savings pool for emergencies, structured as a simple informal agreement or a formal lending circle
- Group travel: sharing costs for medical tourism, explorations of potential relocation destinations, or simply the adventures you've always wanted to take

- A collective voice: advocacy, organizing, or simply bearing witness to each other's lives in a system that'd prefer you to be invisible and isolated

Reflect & Write

- Who are the three to five people you would most want in your circle?

- What would you most want to be honest about with them that you haven't said yet?

- What skills or resources do you bring to a circle like this?

Resources & Further Reading

Community & Mutual Aid

- Mutual Aid Hub: mutualaidhub.org
- The Cohousing Association of the United States: cohousing.org
- Solidarity Economy: solidarityeconomy.us
- TimeBanks USA: timebanks.org
- Buy Nothing Project: buynothingproject.org

Food & Growing

- American Community Gardening Association: communitygarden.org
- Fallen Fruit (foraging maps): fallingfruit.org
- National Center for Home Food Preservation: nchfp.uga.edu
- Free permaculture education: freepermaculture.com

Health & Healthcare

- ACA marketplace coverage: healthcare.gov
- Community Health Centers: findahealthcenter.hrsa.gov
- SHIP (Medicare counseling): shiphelp.org
- Open Path Collective (affordable therapy): openpathcollective.org
- GoodRx: goodrx.com

Money & Benefits

- BenefitsCheckUp: benefitscheckup.org
- Social Security Administration: ssa.gov
- National Foundation for Credit Counseling: nfcc.org
- FreeWill (basic estate planning): freewill.com
- CaringInfo (advance directives): caringinfo.org

Purpose & Learning

- AmeriCorps Seniors: americorps.gov

- Coursera (free online learning): coursera.org

- Osher Lifelong Learning Institutes: osherfoundation.org/olli.html

Spirituality & End of Life

- Death Cafe (community conversations about death): deathcafe.com

- The Order of the Good Death: orderofthegooddeath.com

- Insight Timer (free meditation app): insighttimer.com

Crisis & Emergency Services

- 211 (connection to local resources that can help): 211.org

A Final Word

You didn't do it wrong. You did it differently. And 'differently' contains multitudes: courage, creativity, sacrifice, love, and a refusal to let the economy define your worth. The task now is not to play catch-up with a system that was never designed for you. It's to build the life you actually want, with the people you actually love, in a world that desperately needs exactly what you have to offer.

— The GenX Retirement Twist

Published in 2026 by Elsie Gilmore (elsiegilmore.com)

Also by Elsie Gilmore:
How to Find Joy in a Capitalist Hellscape
Buy it on Bookshop: https://bookshop.org/a/104231/9798990872806
Or here howtofindjoybook.com

Check out the YouTube channel "The GenX Retirement Twist"
https://www.youtube.com/@ElsieGilmore/